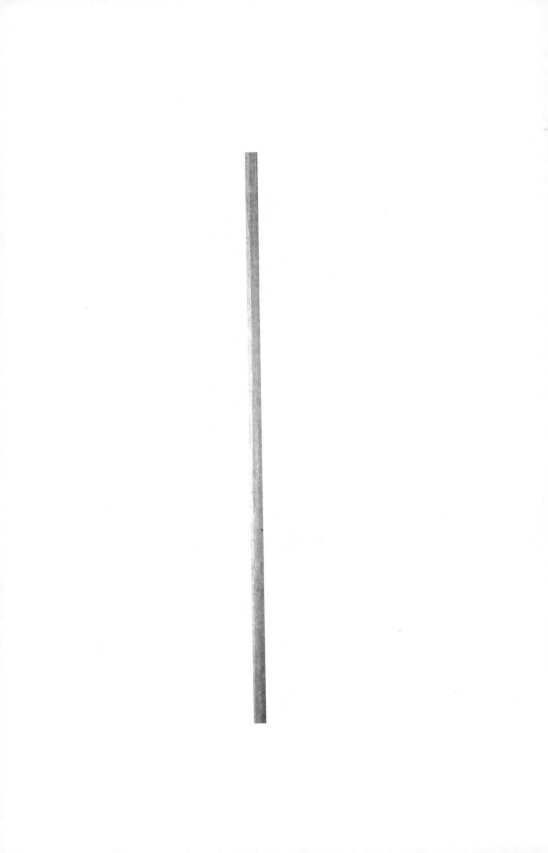

The Challenge of the Mountains
The Canadian Rockies -the Playground of America
ISSUED BY THE
CANADIAN PACIFIC RAILWAY

GOLF LINKS AND CLUB HOUSE, BANFF SPRINGS HOTEL
AND BOW RIVER, BANFF, ALBERTA.

The Challenge of the Mountains

"MOUNTAINS, wherever you find them, have qualities of their own; there is an immense variety of type and of charm, but in all this variety of beauty of mountain scenery there are no mountains which combine grace, and, at the same time, boldness of form with forest and with water more beautifully blended than the Canadian Rockies." (Sir Martin Conway.)

"Europe has its Switzerland, famous throughout the world for the splendor and magnificence of its mountain scenery, which has lured thousands of travelers because of its variety and charm, as well as because of its accessibility. Its scenery is unchangingly beautiful, and the Alpine heights retain a ceaseless fascination for

Banff Springs Hotel, Banff, Alberta.

Mount Assiniboine, (11,860 feet), near Banff, Alberta.

the mountaineer. Yet we turn with wonder and admiration to our own Switzerland. The paradise of our continent lies among the rugged Rocky mountains of Canada. For miles and miles the train glides at their base, showing new wonders at every turn—the wonderful and fascinating glaciers; the number and enormity of the majestic ranges; the sharp precipices; the beautiful snowy peaks; the deep green forests; the lovely clear lakes and peaceful valleys. The Canadian Government has set aside over 6,000 square miles of this region as a national park, and the Canadian Pacific Railway Company has built a number of hotels and chalets, each rivaling the other for comfort, service and fine location. The average traveller, however, spends too little time in this attractive country, as a rule only stopping off for a day or so between trains; while a stay of two or three days should be made at each of the resorts in order to fully note the ever-varying changes of light and shadow, the glorious sunsets; and, the rare experience of visiting the ice caves in the glaciers, in midsummer."—Miss Ilma Schadee, in the "Springfield Republican."

The New York "Tribune" says: "It is not generally known that within four days' journey of New York City there are waiting for the sight-seer and scientific investigator some of the grandest and most impressive glacial streams in the world. Nothing in Switzerland is to be found more beautiful than the glaciers of the Canadian Rockies and Selkirks, and one of the chief attractions of the trip is the fact that one may journey there and back in civilized luxury, and while enjoying the scenes, at the very noses of the wonderful glaciers themselves, be comfortable and remain in close touch with the world."

The Canadian Pacific Railway line, above all others, merits the much-used description, "The scenic line of the world." From Calgary to Vancouver, a distance of six hundred and forty-two miles, the beauty and grandeur of the scenery is continuous. That "there is not a dull or uninteresting minute all the way" is the opinion of all who have made the journey.

Unfortunately, the average tourist is all too prone to stop over only between trains and thus catch but a hurried glance of these glorious peaks, which is regrettable, inasmuch as frequently the greater beauty is missed entirely, though thousands claim that travelling through these mountains without leaving the train has been the most enjoyable event and the greatest scenic treat of their lives.

In the mountain ranges, lakes and valleys of this district are not only the scenic beauties and wonders of Switzerland duplicated on a much wider and grander scale but there is added a diversity of climate noted for its purity of air, its freedom from malaria and an almost total absence of extremes of heat and cold.

Frank Yeigh in his book "Through the Heart of Canada," writes "The transition from the rolling sea of fertile lands to the sea of mountains, is dramatic in the extreme. From the foothills of the Rockies at Calgary to the mouth of the Fraser Canyon the splendid trains of the Canadian Pacific Railway curve to the tune the rivers have set, along the circuitous Bow, along the turbulent Kicking Horse, along and across the broad-breasted Columbia, along the

Canadian Alpine Club in Camp in the Rocky Mountains.

glacial waters of the Illecillewaet, along the blue-green Thompson, until its identity is lost in the yellow Fraser."

The Rockies are visible before Calgary is reached. Mightier and mightier they appear until the Gap, which is the eastern entrance to this mountain world, is reached. Here the track takes a sharp turn and on either side loom skywards the glorious peaks, and the passenger realizes that he has reached Nature's wonderland. Exshaw, the cement town, is passed; then the Three Sisters, a trinity of noble peaks, are seen, immovable, beautiful in their purity, peaceful in their solitude, steadfast in their guard. Like sentinels apart from their compeers, they seem to the traveller to hold eternal watch and ward over the wonders of the marvellous regions through which he is to pass.

Cascade Mountain is a few miles away from the railway track. At its base are the anthracite mines of Bankhead, operated by the Canadian Pacific Railway Company, which supply the country from Winnipeg to Vancouver with hard coal. The powers of the eye

The Gap, or Eastern Entrance to the Canadian Rockies.

are greatly increased, and, to one fresh from the plains, things yet afar off appear quite near. However, the traveller gradually understands his mistake, and the track following the course of the Bow River, turns sharply to the west just as the lowest spurs are reached, and arrives at Banff.

Earl Grey Pass, near Windermere Valley, B.C.

Banff and the Canadian Rockies

BANFF, for romantic situation, stands perhaps unrivalled in America. In its rock ribbed enclosure it is comparatively free from the high winds and dust storms so common in some other resorts at certain seasons.

Located on the south bank of the Bow River near the mouth of the Spray, a wonderful site of remarkable beauty, is the Banff Springs Hotel, of the Canadian Pacific Hotel System. The refinement of its appointments, and the completeness of detail marking the whole establishment, makes this splendid hotel rank among the finest hotels to be found anywhere. The excellence of the cuisine—a characteristic of the Canadian Pacific service—is enhanced by the magnificent outlook down the Bow River Valley.

Bow River Valley and Banff Springs Hotel, Banff, Alberta.

Swimming Pool, Hot Springs, Banff, Alberta.

Banff Hot Springs possess wonderful curative properties for rheumatic and kindred ailments. There are several important springs, the best known of these being the Cave and Basin, where the best of bathing facilities are afforded. The Cave is reached by a delightful drive of about a mile along a winding, pine bordered road up the valley of the Bow River to the base of Sulphur Mountain.

The Cave itself is covered in by a natural roof of rock and is fed by water from the springs further up the mountains. The curious deposits of sulphur about its roof make it well worth a visit. The temperature of the water in the adjoining natural basin where the bathers congregate, is 114.3 degrees Fahrenheit. Connected with the Banff Springs Hotel there are also fine bathing facilities; a new concrete swimming pool has just been completed, 120 feet by 60 feet, which is protected by awnings. Sixty dressing rooms and other facilities make this one of the finest swimming pools in America.

Buffalo at Banff, Alberta.

THE FAUNA OF THE PARK.

A band of buffalo, relics of the countless thousands which once ruled the central plains of North America, occupy an enclosure near the town. With them are a number

Golf on the Picturesque Links at Banff, Alberta.

of elk and moose, together with other specimens of the wild life of the Northern plains and woods.

THE GOLF LINKS AT BANFF, ALBERTA.

An additional attraction at Banff this year, is the magnificent new golf links. Golf enthusiasts who have played the game on the ordinary country club links will find the sport at Banff even more interesting. Here the environments are such as no country club could hope to duplicate. Nestling among the mountains, completely surrounded by gigantic peaks and with the glacier fed Bow River flowing throughout its length, the course lies at an elevation of 5,000 feet, Nature making it not only the highest course on the American continent, but one of surpassing beauty. For the

Club House on Golf Links at Banff, Alberta.

Station at Banff, Alberta.

tourist, golf at Banff has many attractions. Not only is there the peculiar charm of the links themselves, but there is also the exhilaration of the mountain climate.

The climate of Banff is Alpine in character, but it is distinctly drier than the Swiss Alps and has the advantage of having more sunshine. Yet it is seldom ever sultry. This charming town bears a strong resemblance to St. Moritz in the upper Engadine part of Switzerland and the Paracelsus Spring at St. Moritz has the same elevation as the main spring at Banff.

During the summer season the animal cages near the Banff Museum are a continual source of delight to visitors. Here in their steel barred enclosures are fine specimens of black bear, mountain lions, and all of the other big game which are to be found in the Canadian Rockies. The Museum itself contains splendidly preserved exhibits of the game and also of the fish and bird life to be found within the Park. Indian relics are shown and also pieces of Indian workmanship of more than ordinary interest. To the geologist, and the naturalist, the Museum is one of the main points of interest throughout the season. For the botanical student the flora of the district present a wide

Animal Cages, Banff, Alberta.

field for research. Here the profusion and variety of wild flowers is greater than in any other part of the continent. Almost every known species of wild flower can be found within a short distance of the Banff Springs Hotel, making the district one good to live in,—a district where "edelweiss and heather, forget-me-nots and wood anemones, blue-bells and ferns convert all the valleys into flower gardens."

In the Aviary there are some

two hundred specimens of the bird life of the continent. Of the pheasant family alone there are many varieties, among them being Japanese Golden, Japanese Copper, Mongolians, English Silver, English Ringnecks, Prince of Wales, Rieves, Lady Amherst and Common. The eagle cage is also a great attraction to all visitors. Many other specimens of birds are to be found in the Park, and they are all interesting.

Without doubt the Museum and grounds are one of the most attractive and interesting spots in the Park, the many exhibits appealing alike to young and old.

Bow River Falls, Banff, Alberta.

LAKE MINNEWANKA.

From Banff to Lake Minnewanka is nine miles, the drive skirting Cascade Mountain and following Devil's Head River until the precipitous sides of Devil's Head Canyon are crossed by a rustic bridge. The lake is sixteen miles long, with a width of from one to two miles. Here a launch can be chartered by visitors at the rate of $1.00 per head, for parties of five or over. This interesting trip usually occupies three hours. Fishing tackle, boats, etc., may be procured, this being a favorite resort for anglers. A cluster of

Lake Minnewanka, near Banff, Alberta.

Spiral Drive, Tunnel Mountain, Banff, Alberta.

Hoodoos (natural concrete pillars), and the Devil's Gap, on the way to Ghost River, are among the points of interest in this locality.

Other good opportunities for boating are had on the Vermillion lakes, an enlargement of the Bow River. There are lovely stretches of water and they give the visitor unrivalled views of the giants that surround them. Boats can be obtained at low cost and many a pleasant afternoon can be spent in this manner.

The carriage drives radiating from Banff are numerous and beautiful in the extreme. Six livery barns well supplied with saddle horses and carriages, cater to the tourists and others for trips to the many points of interest to which the roads and trails lead. Outfitting stores of all kinds furnish supplies to the residents or camping parties at reasonable prices.

Travelling over the carriage roads and trails extending in all directions from Banff is one of the best ways of seeing the real wonders of this incomparable district. Of the shorter drives "the Loop" is a beautiful roadway around the Bow Valley, in full view of the superb Bow Falls—distance about seven miles—skirting the base of Mount Rundle, to the banks of the Bow River. Another pretty drive is along the north side of the Vermillion lakes, as far west as Edith Pass, from where a beautiful and entirely new view of Mount Edith is obtained. This drive requires about three hours and can be included in a trip to the Cave and Basin.

Tunnel Mountain affords another delightful drive to the visitor.

A spiral roadway has been cut through a charming wood and from the summit the views up and down the valley of the Bow are superb.

Of the longer trails that have been opened, probably the most important is that up Brewster Creek, at the head of which is a huge glacier. This is the nearest glacier to Banff, and can be made in a day by pack train. A day could be spent here and another making the return journey to Banff, giving an ideal three day trip.

For those who wish to go still further from the railway, there is a new trail from Lake Minnewanka, west through Aylmer Pass and down the Ghost River, returning to the Lake by way of the Devil's Gap. There is also another magnificent trail from the Spray Lakes to Kananaskis Lake. The first of these trips requires about a week while two weeks can be profitably spent on the second. Both trails open up magnificent country for the fisherman and sportsman.

For the motor car enthusiast, Banff will soon be attainable by the most wonderful automobile road in the world. This road is now being built by the Dominion Government, the British Columbia Government and the Canadian Pacific Railway. It starts at Calgary and runs through the Mountains to Banff. Here it branches off through the beautiful Vermillion Pass to connect with a road already in existence running from Golden to Cranbrook on the Crow's Nest Pass line of the C.P.R. From here there is a road to Macleod and from that point there is connection with Calgary making a six hundred mile automobile road which when completed will be a magnificent scenic highway.

Truly Banff was born among wonderful environments. The very fact that it is in the centre of the Canadian National Rocky Mountain Park is evidence of the scenic perfectness of its location.

Bow River, Canadian Rockies.

Indians Horse Racing at Banff, Alberta.

This is the largest National government-owned playground in the world, and contains more than 6000 square miles of territory, within which far-flung boundaries there is contained the world's most magnificent scenery. It is a region "unparalleled for majestic mountain ranges, immense ice caps and glaciers, falls and Cascades."

Llewellyn Brown, in the "Standard," says:—"Globe-trotters tell us that 'earth has not anything to show more fair' than that which is to be seen amidst the glories of the Canadian Rockies."

"On every hand you see Nature's handiwork, majestic and sublime. The mighty convulsion that belched up the Rockies, in the gray dawn of history, has left behind it marks which tell us of the magnitude of that great catastrophe. The chiselling effects of the master sculptor are here seen on a magnificent scale, as ages of ice and snow have wrought out the divine plan in æons of time."

Katherine Louise Smith in "Travel" says, of the Park, "New beauties are being constantly discovered by mountain climbers and nature lovers who explore its recesses. It is a place where scenic wonders unfold as in a kaleidoscope, while the pure and exhilarating air fills all who breathe it with vigor. There are heights no man has conquered, a chaos of mountains peak on peak, that change with every ray of light. There are glaciers that sparkle in the sun and valleys that lie in deep shadow. There are rivers, mysterious canons, lakes and tarns—such a plentitude of God's riches that man is lost in their glory."

Lake Louise and Lakes in the Clouds

A RIDE of thirty-four miles by railway through a wonderland of mountain scenery brings one to Laggan, the station for Lake Louise and the Lakes in the Clouds. Carriages meet the trains at Laggan and from here a drive of two and a half miles up a pine girt road takes the traveller to Lake Louise—the most winsome spot in the whole Canadian Rockies. Here charmingly situated on the very verge of the water and in the midst of the evergreen wood the Canadian Pacific Railway has built a magnificent chateau facing the Lake. Everything about the chateau is in good taste. The rooms are large and airy, the service is excellent and the cuisine perfect, and the view from the broad verandahs, across the flower decked lawns, is captivating in the extreme.

Chateau, Lake Louise, Lakes in the Clouds, near Laggan, Alberta.

The growth of interest in this wonderful region has been very rapid. A few years ago, about 1890, a small log house was sufficient to accommodate the visitors who came to pay homage to the matchless scenery of Lake Louise. Each year, however, brought people from all parts of the earth in ever-increasing numbers, and every season the accommodation had to be increased, so that the little house was soon replaced by a larger building; since then wings have been added, remodeling has taken place, and

Path around Lake Louise.

to-day is seen the splendid chalet with all its modern equipment.

Guides and ponies for excursions or short camping trips can be arranged for at the hotel office and also Swiss guides for mountain climbing. The Chateau is open for guests from June 10th till September 30th, and is operated on the American plan, the rates being $4.00 per day and upward

Lake Louise lies at an elevation of 5,645 feet, and is shut in on every side by rocky, snow-capped heights, offering a picture of perfect peace. Mr. Edward Whymper has compared it to Lake Oeshinen, in Switzerland, but has declared it "is more picturesque

Dining Room, Lake Louise Chateau, near Laggan, Alberta.

Laggan, Alberta, the Station for Lake Louise.

ana has more magnificent environments." It is about a mile and a half long and a half-mile broad, while its depth is over two hundred feet.

Of the beauty of this remarkable lake there is no divided opinion; every visitor to its shore sings its praises, and it is acknowledged by the most competent judges to be one of the great masterpieces in Nature's picture gallery. As a gem of composition and coloring it has no rival. At every hour of the day the view is ever-changing with the shadows. This is especially true of the early morning and evening hours. Walter Dwight Wilcox, F.R.G.S., in his charming book, "The Rockies of Canada," describes the colorings of Lake Louise as follows: "It is impossible to tell or paint the beautiful colors, the kaleidosopic

Beautiful Lake Louise.

change of light and shade under such conditions. They are so exquisite that we refuse to believe them even in their presence; so subtle in change, so infinite in variety, that memory fails to recall their varying moods. I have seen twenty shades of green and several of blue in the waters of Lake Louise at one time." It is the most perfect picture in the vast gallery of Nature's masterpieces.

Lake Louise is noted for its avalanches and it is not uncommon to hear the thunder of several of these in one day.

Two miles across the boulder-covered glacier lake there begins to rise southward the forefront of the great glaciers. Thence the ice slants away upwards, until it reaches a depth of possibly five hundred feet of solid blue and green, to where it is fed by continuous avalanches from the endless groups of enormous heights beyond. At the upper end of this brow rises a stern black wall to a height of fully half a mile, over which the avalanches thunder. This wall is five miles away, yet looks to be but one, because of the clearness of the atmosphere.

Above this black avalanche wall there gradually rises, like the roof of the universe, the pure white snowfield on Mount Victoria to a height of over ten thousand feet. Joining with Victoria in forming this ice field are the towering heights of Lefroy, Beehive, Whyte, Niblock, St. Piran, Castle Crags and many other lofty peaks.

There are good trails from Lake Louise to the other Lakes in the Clouds. Mirror Lake has no visible outlet, its waters escaping through an underground channel to Lake Louise, 1,000 feet below. The waters of this lake rise or fall as the inflowing

Lakes in the Clouds, Laggan, Alberta

Chateau Lake Louise, near Laggan, Alberta.

stream pours its flood into the lake more or less rapidly than they are carried off. Lake Agnes, another of the Lakes in the Clouds, is situated amid scenes of the wildest beauty. On the side, like senti-nels, stand Mounts Whyte and Niblock, grim and silent; and the irregular peaks, running back tell of violent eruption in that great and terrible day of upheaval far back in the misty ages of the earth's infancy. A little way down the valley Nature smiles, not broadly, but none the less sweetly; for here among the mosses are found the forget-me-nots, the wood anemones, the blue bells of the Scottish Highlands, the ferns, the Alpine edelweiss (the bridal flower of the Swiss mountaineer) and the heather, that reminds the sons and daughters of Bonnie Scotland of their native hills.

To the east of Laggan run two mountain valleys, both of which are famous for their exquisite scenery Paradise Valley, the nearer to Lake Louise, lies between Mount Sheol and Mount Temple, while the valley of the Ten Peaks, as its name implies, is sentineled by ten great peaks, and holds at its head Moraine Lake. There is good trout fishing in Moraine Lake, which is reached from Lake Louise.

This year the visitor to Lake Louise will have the opportunity of travelling over several new trails which were built during the season of 1911. Among these is a new promenade trail around the Eastern side of Lake Louise. This path connects with the old route around the Western side of the lake and permits of the full circuit of the waters being made. This trail skirts the lake at an elevation of about 100 feet. Benches and rest houses have been placed at intervals, from which the ever-changing color effects of the waters may be observed to great advantage.

There is also a new trail to the Upper Lakes in the Clouds. From here the trail has been continued to Little Beehive Mountain,

Riding is Popular at Lake Louise.

from where wonderful views can be had of the three Lakes in the Clouds and the Bow Valley with its array of peaks. The more ambitious sightseer may from the Little Beehive continue up to the top of Mount St. Piran.

Still another new trail is that leading up to the top of and over Sentinel Pass. This Pass connects Paradise Valley with the Valley of the Ten Peaks. At Moraine Lake it connects with the carriage road already in existence to Laggan Station and Lake Louise. In Paradise Valley this trail allows of a visit to the celebrated Giants' Steps Falls a beautiful cascade or succession of falls.

Six miles from Laggan is the summit of the Rockies and here is the Great Divide, 5,296 feet above sea level. It is marked by a rustic arch spanning a stream, under which the waters divide, by one of those curious freaks with which Nature occasionally diverts herself, into two little brooks which have curiously different fates, though they have a common origin. The waters that deviate to the east eventually mingle with the ice-cold tides of Hudson Bay, while the rivulet that turns to the west adds its mite to the volume of the Pacific.

The Great Divide.

Spiral Tunnels near Field, B.C.

BETWEEN Hector, near the summit of the Rockies, and Field, at the base of Mount Stephen, is encountered one of the greatest pieces of engineering work of this century. When the Canadian Pacific Railway was first completed through to the Pacific Coast the grade at this point was a particularly heavy one. In the early days of the railway this grade rendered the operation of trains over this section of the road unusually difficult, not only on account of the power necessary to haul the trains over the steep incline, but also on account of the precautions that had to be taken to ensure safety alike to passengers and equipment. As the volume of the railway's business grew it was decided that something had to

Spiral Tunnels near Field, B.C.

Spiral Tunnels from First Panorama.

be done to eliminate the necessity for running the trains over the "Big Hill." It was decided to overcome the grade by a series of spiral tunnels. The adoption of this scheme marked a new epoch in American engineering, this being the first application of the spiral curve principle made on this continent.

Roughly speaking the work that the Canadian Pacific Railway has done at this point is as follows: Firstly, it has added several miles to its track. Secondly, it has built two bridges over the same river, the Kicking Horse. Thirdly, it has excavated three-quarters of a million feet of rock, and finally it has bored one and one-quarter miles of tunnel in gigantic mountains. And the result is: a reduction in grade of from 4.5 per cent. to 2.2 per cent. To the uninitiated the outlay hardly seems to justify the result, but listen to the expert.

"This work has resulted in the cutting down of the number of locomotives required on the average train making the trip over the line at this point from four to two. It has altogether eliminated the danger attending the negotiation of the heavy grade, and instead of being able to make only four or five miles an hour, as the four engines used to do on the old track, the two engines used now can make twenty miles an hour

The conformation of the new track is most peculiar. Coming from the east the road first enters the western corkscrew tunnel of 3,200 feet, under Cathedral Mountain. Emerging from the tunnel twist the track runs back east across the Kicking Horse River, and then enters the eastern spiral tunnel of 2,910 feet under Mount Ogden, and after describing an elliptic curve emerges to again cross the Kicking Horse westward. The whole thing is a perfect maze, the railway doubling back upon itself twice, tunneling under mountains and crossing the river twice in order to cut down the grade.

Some facts regarding the work done are as follows: length of two tunnels, 1¼ miles; length of cutting, outside of tunnels, 7 miles; increase in length of track, 4¼ miles; reduction in grade, from 4.5 to 2.2; approximate cost of work, $1,500,000; number of men employed, about 1,000. Time of work, twenty months; rock removed, about 650,000 cubic yards; 75 carloads of dynamite used. The cost of this quantity of explosives alone came to over $250,000.

Field, Emerald Lake and Yoho Valley

A T Field the Kicking Horse River, for a short distance, flows across broad, level flats that are only covered when the water is high. The place itself is a prosperous little village, but is dwarfed into insignificance by the splendid mountains that hem it in. On one side is Mount Burgess; on the other Mount Stephen, one of the grandest of all the Rockies. Field is the gateway to the wonderful Yoho Valley, and the headquarters for mountaineers of the more ambitious type. Here is located the spacious and comfortable Mount Stephen House of the Canadian Pacific Hotel System.

This hotel enjoys a splendid reputation for its service, and guests

Mount Stephen House, at Field, B.C.

will find here one of the most interesting and enjoyable resorts in the mountains.

Looking from the shoulder of Mount Burgess or Mount Stephen the valley seems narrow, the river a mere stream, and the dwellings in the village dolls' houses. From below, Mount Stephen fills all the view; so rounded, so symmetrical, the spectator hardly realizes at first that he has before him a rock mass towering 10,000 feet above sea level and 6,500 feet above the valley.

The lower slopes of the mountain have one spot well worth

Mount Stephen and Field, B.C.

visiting, the fossil bed, where for 150 yards the side of the mountain, for a height of 300 or 400 feet, has slid forward and broken into a number of shaly, shelving limestone slabs, exposing innumerable fossils.

From Field is a delightful drive of seven miles round the spurs of Mount Burgess to the beautiful Emerald Lake. The road leads through a splendid spruce forest. In one place the road has been cut straight as an arrow for a mile in length; Snow Peak Avenue this stretch is called. At Emerald Lake is a charming chalet operated by the Canadian Pacific Railway where tourists may find excellent accommodation at the very entrance to the wonderful Yoho Valley.

Emerald Lake is one of the most fascinating spots in this wonderful mountain region. Replete with lovely pictures, the coloring of Emerald Lake is rich and vivid, the contrast between the water and the trees being very striking. The lake appears as an irridescent scintillating expanse of water, mirroring four great snow capped peaks that rise from its depths.

The Beautiful Road between Field and Emerald Lake.

One of the most interesting of the short excursions to be made from Field is a walk of two and a half miles to the Natural Bridge, spanning the Kicking Horse River. Here a series of vertical rock ridges which at one time formed a barrier across the Kicking Horse River, have been undermined and cut through by the action of the

Natural Bridge, near Field, B.C.

water, which rushes with great force through a narrow gorge only a few feet wide, while an overhanging mass of rock forms the bridge itself.

Emerald Lake is half way to the Yoho Valley, one of the most beautiful mountain valleys in the world.

It is a most delightful experience to ride from Emerald Lake through the Yoho Valley and stay at the comfortable camps provided by the Canadian Pacific Railway Company for tourists. Every person who has taken this trip is enthusiastic regarding the many beautiful sights and scenes visited. On this riding trip will be seen mighty glaciers, their surfaces lit up and flecked with many hues in the sunlight, and charming cascades, their waters leaping, in a filmy, threadlike line, 800 feet or more. Thick woods shut out the summit of the pass, but part asunder to grant a glimpse of Summit Lake, a stretch of water 1,800 feet above Emerald Lake.

C.P.R. Camps, Yoho Valley

Emerald Lake Chalet and Mount Burgess.

The camps in the Yoho Valley are models of comfort. Picturesquely situated under the shadows of the mountains a stay of three or four days at one of them brings one in close touch with Nature. Here in the daytime you can find a hundred and one ways to amuse yourself. You can photograph the mountains at first hand. You can fish the foaming mountain streams for trout. You can explore the glaciers or you can hit the trail into new fastnesses. "And who shall adequately sing the song of the hill trail? The winding way, turf-carpeted, through the forest aisles; the

Summit Lake, Yoho Valley.

breath-catching glimpses of guardian giants, the closer acquaintance with glacial rivers and wayward brooks, the greetings of the trailside flowers, the greetings too, of whistling marmots and lazy porcupines, and of all the varied life of the high hills." Truly this is life. Lucky indeed is he who can leave the world of cities and commune with Nature, under the drifted skies of Yoho Valley.

A short distance from Emerald Lake is Lookout Point from where is secured a superb view of the surrounding country. Ahead for twenty miles the glacier-girt Yoho Valley unfolds its marvelous panorama,—the fairest corner of the earth. It is a living verdant garden walled in with eternal rocks and snows. Throughout its length a white foaming river runs. From the great plateaus of snow countless waterfalls leap down the cliffs to join the river below. Greatest of them all is the giant Takakkaw, which plunges from a height of twelve hundred feet over a

Emerald Lake.

Takakkaw Falls, Yoho Valley.

tremendous rock wall. Its voice of thunder awakens a thousand echoes in the valley. "Takakkaw" in the Indian tongue, means "It is wonderful," and so it is.

But the Takakkaw are not the only falls of the Yoho.

All up the valley other cascades are seen or heard. The hills are crowned with glaciers, and the water melted from them seeks the shortest way to the valley, even at the cost of a plunge of hundreds of feet. Perhaps the most fascinating are the Laughing Falls. Their leap is only 200 feet, but their waters seem to laugh with glee as they go, and their milk-white flood smiles delightfully through the dark evergreens around. Further up the valley, on the left branch of the forked stream, are the

Twin Falls, an almost unique phenomenon, and as beautiful as it is unexpected. Over a cliff five hundred feet high, the melting glacier falls in twin cataracts to the base of the rock wall where they unite in a series of cascades, which plunge ultimately down a superb gorge with perpendicular walls over a hundred feet high.

The excellent camps and good trails of the Yoho Valley make a trip through the vale one of the most delightful mountain rides in America. A great glacier, too, far larger even than the famous Illecillewaet Glacier of the Selkirks, overhangs the right-hand fork of the valley. The

Twin Falls, Yoho Valley.

Wapta Glacier, as it is named, is part of the great Waputekh ice field guarded by Mount Gordon, Mount Balfour and the broken crags of Trolltinderne (The Elfin's Crown).

At the forks of the Yoho Valley a shelter has been provided for visitors and there are many who take advantage of it

The trip round the valley from Emerald Lake can be made in a day. The return to Field may be varied by crossing the Burgess Pass, which is unquestionably one of the finest mountain rides in the world, and should be taken by every lover of mountain scenery. From this lofty trail Emerald Lake is seen thousands of feet below, with the Emerald Range rising beyond, while on the other hand Mounts Cathedral, Stephen and Dennis and the Ottertail Range excite admiration. From this eminence a zig-zag path leads down by easy stages to Mount Stephen House.

During the year 1910, the carriage road from Field up the Yoho Valley, leading to Takakkaw Falls, was completed. The most difficult portions of the road—a couple of switch-backs—were put in to make the grade of the ascent easier. From the summit of the second switch-back a magnificent view of the river valley below and Cathedral Mountain in the background is obtained. From this point it is intended to construct a foot-path through the undergrowth to the river canyon, about one hundred yards distant, and to have a number of rustic seats placed for the convenience and accommodation of tourists who will avail themselves of the opportunity of visiting this wonderful view. Tourists from all parts of the world have pronounced this valley one of the most beautiful they have ever seen and the carriage road one of the best of mountain roads.

At Golden, near Field, is seen the model Swiss Village of "Edelweiss," built by the Canadian Pacific Railway for their Swiss guides. For many years the C.P.R. have followed the practise of bringing over from Europe a number of experienced guides who are stationed at the various Rocky mountain resorts to aid those desiring to try mountain climbing. Formerly these guides returned to Switzerland

Swiss Village of "Edelweiss", near Golden, B.C.

Mountaineering Party at Lake Hector, near the Great Divide,
in the Canadian Rocky Mountains.

at the close of each season, but beginning this year they will make
Canada their permanent home, residing at "Edelweiss." These
guides are always at the service of guests at the various hotels,
where arrangements for their services can be made.

The Canadian Pacific Railway along with the Alpine Club of
Canada has done much to popularize mountain climbing in the
Canadian Rockies. The Alpine Club has been especially active,

its annual camps at the various scenic points between Banff and Glacier being largely attended. Many representatives from various other clubs frequently visit Emerald Lake, Lake Louise and the other mountain resorts, where every opportunity is afforded them to enjoy this invigorating and beneficial form of recreation.

Mountaineering is the greatest sport in the world. No other play is so joyous in its anticipation nor so stimulating in its realization. It brings you close to the high places of the world and gives the further compensation of physical fitness. There is no other recreation which, in all its aspects of surroundings and exercise, will bring about such a fast regeneration of worn out nerves, tired brains and flabby muscles.

Swiss Guides in Canadian Rockies.

Speaking of the Canadian Rockies, Dr. T. G. Longstaff, the distinguished mountaineer says, "A visit of three months in Canada leads me to remark that no mountaineer can withstand the attractions of the Canadian Rockies. In the Canadian Rockies and Selkirks there is a country awaiting for recognition, which I believe is destined to become the playground of the world. In no other mountain region of the globe do peak and cliff, snowfield and glacier, alpland and forest, lake, cataract and stream form such a perfect combination as is to be found not in one, but in hundreds of places in these glorious ranges."

Not only men, but also women are falling victims to the alluring attractions of mountain climbing. They have come to the realization of the fact that no other sport embodies such features of health and attractiveness and every year more and more women are making their first ascents and joining the ranks of the experienced mountaineers.

The great field of action is alone sufficient to attract the mountaineer. As the New York Sun says, "There are chances for the mountain climber in the Canadian Rockies that surpass almost anything on earth. There are still many peaks that have never been climbed, and there are relatively few that have recognized and usual courses of ascent, even those nearest the railway."

Glacier House and Great Glacier

NESTLING in a niche of the narrow valley, a few rods from the railway, and surrounded by the beautiful evergreen trees that everywhere thrive in this region, is a charming hotel, the Glacier House, which has become so popular that the Canadian Pacific Railway Company has found it necessary to enlarge the original structure, and erect new buildings. General Hamilton wrote in the guests' book at the hotel: "My wife and I have travelled for nearly forty years all over the world, and are both agreed the scenery at Glacier House is the finest we have seen in Europe, Asia, Africa or America."

First to attract the tourist is the Great Glacier of the Selkirks,

Glacier House, Glacier, B.C.

which crowds its tremendous head down the mountain gorge, within thirty minutes' walk of the hotel. At the left Sir Donald rears his mighty peak more than a mile and a half above the railway. A mountain rivulet rushes down the abruptly rocky sides of the mountain opposite the hotel, and a trail has been cut up the steep incline to a spot beside the rushing stream where a rustic summer house has been erected. The effect is novel and pleasing. The waters from this stream have been utilized to supply the hotel and fountains that play in the foreground. All the streams here are simply ice water from the glaciers. A tower has been erected near the annex of the hotel, on which is a large telescope commanding a view of the great glacier and surrounding objects.

The Great Glacier is nearly two miles from the hotel, but among such gigantic surroundings looks much nearer. It is the centre of a group of glaciers embracing more than one hundred and fifty-seven square miles, and the hoary head seen from the hotel is one

The Great Glacier, Glacier, B.C.

of several outlets. The great ice peaks and glaciers are truly an interesting study. They intensify the gloomy thick clouds, and burst into glittering silver when the sun shines on them. Later they are robed in the gorgeous colors of the evening; and in the mysterious silent night the moon and the stars look down to see their faces in their glassy surfaces.

The Illecillewaet Glacier, like nearly every other observed glacier in the world, is receding. It is reckoned that the sun drives it back on the average thirty-five feet a year, recovering this much from the bonds of ice. However, after the ice is gone, and the moraine remains, it will be many centuries before the great rocks carried down by the glacier are reduced to dust, and the land thus reclaimed supports renewed vegetation.

The Loops of the Selkirks, near Glacier.

From Glacier House other expeditions of great interest may be made. One trail leads first to the shores of Marion Lake, 1,750 feet above, and two miles distant from the hotel, where a shelter is erected. Splendid views are obtained, on the way, of the range from Eagle Peak to Sir Donald, and a path strikes off for Observation Point, where another shelter is built for those who would dwell on the glories of Rogers' Pass to the northeast and the Illecillewaet Valley to the west. Mount Abbott is a day's climb, but it is an easy one, and should be undertaken by all, for from it a splendid view is obtained of the Asulkan Valley.

From Observation Point an extremely fine view is obtained down the Illecillewaet Valley, along the precipitous sides of which the track makes a descent of 522 feet in seven miles. This feat taxed to the utmost the skill of the engineers, and they accomplished it by means of the famous Loops of the Selkirks, a winding course which the railway has to follow.

First, the track crosses a valley leading from Mount Bonney Glacier. Then it touches, for a moment, the base of Ross Peak. It doubles back to the right for a mile or more and so close are the tracks that a stone might be tossed from one to the other. Next it sweeps around and reaches the slope of Mount Cougar, on the other side of the Illecillewaet, but it has to cross the stream once more before it finally finds a way parallel to the general trend of the valley. The line has made a double "S" in its course, and has cut two long gashes on the mountain side, one above the other.

Observation Tower, Glacier House, Glacier, B.C.

Twenty-two miles from Glacier, the Illecillewaet River runs through the Albert Canyon, a gorge so marvellous that several of the regular trains stop for a few minutes to allow passengers to see its wonders.

Mount Sir Donald, Near Glacier, B.C.

THE GREAT CAVES OF
NAKIMU, NEAR GLACIER, B.C.

These great caves, which were discovered by Charles H. Deutschman, are situated about six miles from Glacier, B.C., at the head of a beautiful valley, the altitude being 1,980 feet from the track and above the snow line. The wonderful caverns are formed by the action of water for ages upon the solid rock, and are a series of chambers with large entrances, the ceilings being polished rock, and varying in height. The main chamber is about 200 feet in height, with a varying width of from 150 to 200 feet. The walls sparkle with the quartz crystals, and myriads of miniature lights are reflected from the darkness.

In other parts the walls are smooth as marble, the harder portions of the formation showing like the rounded pillars of a cathedral dome. No evidence has so far been discovered that any portion of these caverns has ever been used as the habitation of human beings. A visit to these remarkable caves is an interesting day's trip from Glacier, as the scenery from the trail is grand beyond description.

The Canadian Rockies appeal strongest in the summer months, when in most American cities the sun is beating mercilessly down during the long torrid days; then "flee to the Mountains" for that refreshing balm to tired minds and jaded nerves, where the exhilarating air imbues all with new life and energy.

The Canadian Rockies are unique for their abnormally high percentage of sunny days, their corresponding minimum of rain, and

Lookout Point at Caves of Nakimu.

Glacier, B.C., showing the Canadian Pacific Railway, the Station
and the Great Glacier itself.

the entire absence of foggy or misty weather and dew. From the
1st of June to the 1st of October there is practically no rain, except
passing showers of short duration, preceded and succeeded by bright
sunshine.

No greater contrast is it possible for mortals to enjoy than
from the city with its noisy rushing tumult, and the smoky, dusty,
hot streets, prosy stores and dwellings, where man and mammon
reign, to the Canadian Rockies, with their ambient air, blue skies,
fleecy clouds that oft obscure the giant peaks, emerald lakes and
rushing streams of clear pure water. The mountains, from time
immemorial, have always been an inspiration to mankind to higher
thoughts, where he is impressed with the magnitude of the works
of Nature, and the insignificance of the works of man; and inspired
to higher ideals and loftier purposes in life.

Everywhere in the mountains the visitor finds himself in strange
surroundings, and over all stand the majestic snow-tipped peaks,
ever extending a challenge to the newcomer to scale the granite
barrier and view a new world, with its endless combinations of light
and shade, parks and passes and gorges, always pervaded by a
clear electric atmosphere, which is a revelation to persons accustomed
to living in the close, damp air of the lower altitudes.

The Glorious Kootenay

REVELSTOKE is an important centre; from it there is water communication with the rich Kootenay and Boundary districts. It is on the Columbia River, which has made a great bend since the train crossed it at Donald and flowing now south instead of north, is much increased in size. Twenty-eight miles below Revelstoke it expands into the Arrow Lakes, at Arrowhead, and from there well-appointed Canadian Pacific Railway steamboats carry travellers to Nakusp and Robson from which the Slocan, Kootenay, Boundary and Rossland districts are reached.

Down the Arrow Lakes the steamer plies to Nakusp and West Robson, passing, near the head of the lakes, the famous Halcyon Hot Springs. This is a favorite summer resort, having a good hotel, while opposite is Halcyon Peak, 10,400 feet high, and several

City of Nelson, British Columbia.

C.P.R. Boat, near Nelson, B.C.

fine waterfalls. A spur of the Canadian Pacific Railway connects Nakusp with Sandon, on Slocan Lake, in the centre of the silver-lead district, and with Rosebery, to join the steamer that plies down the lake to Slocan City. Here again the rails begin and communicate with Robson, at the end of the Lower Arrow on the west, and with Nelson, on an arm of Kootenay Lake, on the east

The Arrow Lakes steamer has also come the full length from West Robson, 165 miles through splendid mountain scenery, while from West Robson trains run over a short but important line to Trail and Rossland, through one of the richest mining regions in the world. Yet another branch from Robson has been constructed through the Boundary district to Midway and opens up another prosperous mining locality.

The Crows' Nest Branch of the Canadian Pacific Railway ends at Kootenay Landing, and from there to Nelson there is communi-

Halcyon Springs, at Arrow Lake, B.C.

Kootenay Lake Hotel, at Balfour, B.C.

cation by Canadian Pacific Railway steamer. At Balfour, near Nelson, the Canadian Pacific have erected a hotel for tourists, as this district has great natural beauty. A steamboat line has been established from Nelson up Kootenay Lake to Lardo, whence an isolated branch of railway runs thirty-two miles north to Gerrard, and a steamer plies across Trout Lake to Trout Lake City, a matter of seventeen miles, so that every part of Southern British Columbia may be visited. This is a charming country, which is growing each season in popularity; attracting, by its many charms of lake and mountain, tourists who love the fertile stretches in the beautiful valleys, with their nestling fruit farms and the presence of population and industry.

Nelson, the chief city in the Kootenay district, is situated at an altitude of 1,760 feet above the sea level and on the south shore of a splendid stretch of water. It is a charming city to visit and has many attractions, including excellent rainbow trout fishing to offer to anglers.

The Kootenay District has not only singular beauty of its own, but it is also attaining a splendid reputation as a fruit-growing section. Around Nelson are produced splendid apples, plums, cherries and small fruits in large quantities and of delicious flavor. The climate is much milder than in the Canadian Rockies to the north, and the soil is apparently ideal for fruit culture.

Many tourists are now taking the Kootenay trip as an alternative route to the Pacific Coast, and thus seeing Canada's mountains under varying conditions, as the Kootenay has not the rugged grandeur of the Canadian Rockies, but a different fascinating beauty of valley, lake and mountain that appeals because of its varied general attractiveness.

P. A. O'Farrell, the well-known writer says of the Kootenay and Arrow Lakes, "Few people, have any conception of the transcendent beauty and of the riches of the Kootenays. There is nothing half so grand, half so sublime, or half so beautiful in the scenery of Switzerland or the Tyrol. Its river, forest, mountain and lake scenery excel the world, and its climate is the best and most delightfully health giving on this globe."

"All the navies of Europe could manoeuvre for battle on the Arrow or Kootenay Lakes. Slocan Lake could float all the war ships of the world, and Lake Windermere rivals Killarney in enchanting loveliness."

One of the Scenic Features of the Kootenay District.

Vancouver, Victoria and Pacific Coast

STILL another Canadian Pacific hotel is encountered at Sicamous Junction, on Shuswap Lake. From here a branch line of the railway extends southward to the Okanagan Lake, a beautiful sheet of water on which the railway operates a steamship service. The round trip from Sicamous Junction to the foot of the Lake occupies two days and forms a most enjoyable side trip.

Just beyond Ashcroft the Canyon of the Thompson is entered, and the railway follows the river which here rushes forward foaming and churning. At Lytton is met the Fraser River and shortly after is entered the famous Fraser Canyon. This is one of the most beautiful canyons in the world, the river rushing through perpendicular cliffs hundreds of feet in height. For several miles the railway hugs the towering cliffs, passing North Bend, in the very heart of the canyon.

At Yale is felt the balmy air of the Pacific. At Spence's Bridge is a curious Indian cemetery. At Agassiz is a fine Government experimental fruit farm, while five miles away to the north is Harrison Lake, a beautiful spot, with its hot sulphur springs, the visitors to which will find good accommodation at Harrison Springs Hotel.

At Mission Junction the branch line runs to the international boundary, and there joins the Northern Pacific Railroad. By this route Seattle is reached and connection with the Shasta Route for San Francisco and all the Pacific States. The main line, however, keeps on past Westminster Junction (where a branch line leads to Westminster), and arrives at the terminus of the Canadian Pacific Railway at Vancouver.

Vancouver, on the shores of Burrard Inlet, is the largest city in British Columbia, and has one of the finest harbors on the Pacific. The many attractions of Vancouver, and the splendid service of the Canadian Pacific Railway Hotel Vancouver, offer many inducements to visit the numerous points of interest from here.

Vancouver typifies the true enterprising spirit of the West. While comparatively a young city it is making rapid strides forward and is destined to become one of the largest municipalities on the Pacific Coast. In its early days the city was swept by a devastating forest fire, which left destruction in its wake, but

the calamity only resulted in a
temporary set back to the town
and did not prevent it from gain-
ing its present importance as an
industrial and commercial centre.

There are many beauty spots
in the vicinity of Vancouver,
which the tourist. should see.
Chief among these is Stanley
Park a magnificent public playground reservation, wherein the
huge trees, for which British
Columbia is so justly famous, are
one of the feature attractions.
Another beauty spot in the vicinity of Vancouver is the Capilano
Canon where some titanic dis-
turbance has made a deep wound
in the mother earth. At one
point the huge chasm is crossed
by a suspended foot bridge from
which a magnificent view of the
gorge is obtained.

A few hours' steam from
Vancouver is Victoria, the capital
of British Columbia. Across the

Falls Near Vancouver.

Straits of Georgia ply daily the Canadian Pacific Railway steamers "Princess Victoria" and "Princess Charlotte," of the Vancouver-
Victoria-Seattle service, passing through an archipelago of small
islands, comparable to the Thousands Islands of the St. Lawrence,
though with infinitely finer timber.

Canadian Pacific Railway's Hotel Vancouver, at Vancouver, B.C.

Victoria is a city of lovely homes and the seat of the Provincial Government, its Parliament Building being one of the handsomest edifices on the continent. This city is of singular beauty. The magnificent Empress Hotel, one of the latest additions to the splendid Canadian Pacific Hotel System, overlooks the harbor, and for situation and appointments is acknowledged to be one of the finest hotels on the Pacific Coast.

Beacon Hill Park, 300 acres in extent, is no less beautiful than Stanley Park of Vancouver. Numerous other attractions are offered to visitors, including splendid drives, golf and other sports.

The Parliament Building, at Victoria, is acknowledged to be one of the handsomest and most imposing structures on the continent. It is one of the first sights to catch the visitor's eye as he enters the

Foot Bridge spanning the Capilano Canon, near Vancouver, B.C.

Canadian Pacific Railway's Empress Hotel, Victoria, British Columbia.

harbor of Victoria. It stands amid spacious and beautifully-kept lawns, the vivid green of which testifies to the mildness of the climate.

In the Parliament Buildings there are three distinct Museums, namely: in the Agricultural Department, the Mines Department, and in a wing solely devoted to this purpose, there is what is known as the Provincial Museum. This latter contains a most interesting collection of British Columbia fossils, Indian curios and specimens of natural history, and it is said by experts to be one of the most perfect collections of its kind in America.

The Esquimalt & Nanaimo Railway, from Victoria, has some very interesting scenery to offer tourists, as well as excellent fishing and hunting resorts. An important feature of the Railway is that, by its completion to Port Alberni that point is made the most westerly station in North America, with transcontinental connection. It is also the nearest Canadian port to the Orient.

From Vancouver and Victoria connections can be made by steamers with all parts of the world.

The Canadian Pacific Railway Company's Empresses transport passengers swiftly and comfortably to Japan or China. The Canadian-Australian line runs regularly to Honolulu, Fiji, Australia and New Zealand; while if such long journeys are not desired, take a Canadian Pacific Railway steamer up the British Columbia coast to Alaska. The railway has an excellent steamship service to northern points during the summer months, and the run is a popular one, the route winding, throughout practically the whole course, among the countless islands that dot the west coast. This sea voyage through the inland waterways of British Columbia has much of the weirdness and the beauty of other famous places, combined with a peculiar charm of its own. It is distinctive in that it is a salt water trip through a mountainous district, because the islands past which the ships steam can, almost without exception, boast of at least one mountain of good size.

At present the Canadian Pacific Railway operates three boats between Canada and the Orient,—The Empress of Japan, the Empress of India and the Monteagle. Next year this service will be augmented by the addition of two palatial new "Empresses,"—the Empress of Russia and the Empress of Asia. These new steamships are now being built in England and they will be the largest and speediest boats operating on the Pacific ocean. They will be 570 feet long, 68 feet beam, and will have a gross tonnage of 15,000 tons. Speeding across the Pacific ocean at a speed of twenty knots an hour the new boats will be able to cut down the time required for the voyage from Victoria to the Orient to ten days. Each of the new steamships will have accommodation for over 1,200 passengers, and will cost $2,500,000 each. They will be the first merchant steamships to be built with cruiser sterns.

The interiors of the ships will be models of steamship elegance. With the spacious social rooms and deck promenades provided there will be no crowding. The cabins and suites will be unusually large and amongst the new features, instead of the ordinary berths in the cabins there will be bedsteads of brass or wood. There will be writing rooms, a music room, library, cafe, a reception room, a gymnasium, and a big beautiful dining room which will accommodate all the passengers at one sitting.

The vessels will be equipped with every known device for safe navigation, including wireless telegraphy and submarine signal system, and will be driven by turbine engines of 17,000 horse power. The advent of these Ships to the Pacific will add greatly to the pleasure of a trip to Japan and China.

Canadian Pacific Railway's New Pacific Ocean Steamships, Empresses of Asia and Russia.

Canadian Pacific Railway
AGENCIES.

Adelaide...... SOUTH AUS.. Australasian United Steam Nav. Co., Ltd............
Antwerp ..... BELGIUM. Thos. McNeil, Agent................................ 25 Quai Jordaens
Auckland........ N.Z.. Union S. S. Co. of New Zealand, Ltd.................
Baltimore........ MD.. A. W. Robson, Passenger and Ticket Agent........127 East Baltimore St.
Battle Creek.. MICH.. E. C. Oviatt, Traveling Passenger Agent............363 Lake Ave.
Belfast .... IRELAND.. Wm. McCalla, Agent................................ 41 Victoria St.
Bellingham ..... WASH.. W. H. Gordon, Passenger Agent..................... 113 West Holly St.
Berlin ...... GERMANY. International Sleeping Car Co...................... 69 Unter den Linden
Birmingham .... ENG.. W. J. Treadway, Agent............................ 4 Victoria Square
Bombay .... INDIA.. Thos. Cook & Son, Ewart Latham & Co............
Boston........ MASS.. F. R. Perry, General Agent, Passenger Department..... 332 Washington St.
.... G. A. Titcomb, City Passenger Agent............ 332 Washington St.
Brandon .... MAN.. J. E. Proctor, District Passenger Agent...........
Brisbane .... QD.. The British India and Queensland Agency Co., Ltd..
Bristol .... ENG.. A. S. Ray, Agent................................ 18 St. Augustine's Parade
Brussels .... BELGIUM. Thos. Cook & Son................................ 47 Rue de la Madeleine
.... International Sleeping Car Co.................... Nord Station
Buffalo........ N.Y.. G. H. Griffin, City Passenger Agent.............. 302 Main St.
Calcutta ...... INDIA.. Thos. Cook & Son................................ 9 Old Court House St.
.... Gillanders, Arbuthnot & Co....................
Calgary........ ALTA.. R. C. McNeillie, District Passenger Agent........
Canton........ CHINA.. Jardine, Matheson & Co..........................
Chicago........ ILL.. Geo. A. Walton, General Agent, Passenger Department. 224 South Clark St.
Cincinnati ...... OHIO.. A. J. Blaisdell, General Agent, Passenger Department.... 436 Walnut St.
Cleveland ...... OHIO.. Geo. A. Clifford, City Passenger Agent...Cor. Superior and West Third Sts.
Cologne ..... GERMANY. Thos. Cook & Son................................ 1 Domhof
.... International Sleeping Car Co.................... Central Station
Colombo ...... CEYLON.. Thos. Cook & Son; Bois Brothers & Co............
Detroit .... MICH.. A. E. Edmonds, District Passenger Agent......... 7 Fort Street W.
Duluth .... MINN.. James Maney, Gen. Pass. Agent, D. S. S. & A. Ry.. Manhattan Bldg.
Frankfort .... GERMANY. International Sleeping Car Co.................... 47 Kaiserstrasse
Glasgow ..... SCOTLAND.. Thomas Russell, Agent.......................... 120 St. Vincent St.
Halifax .... N.S.. J. D. Chipman, City Passenger and Freight Agent..... 57 George St.
Hamburg .... GERMANY. C. F. A. Flügge, Agent........................... 8 Alsterdamm
Hamilton .... ONT.. J. Merrinan, City Passenger Agent........Cor. King and James Sts.
Hobart ...... TASMANIA.. Union S. S. Co. of New Zealand, Ltd.............
Hongkong ...... CHINA.. D. W. Craddeck, General Traffic Agent, China, etc...
Honolulu .... H.I.. Theo. H. Davies & Co., Ltd.....................
Kansas City ..... MO.. Ed. Merchant, Traveling Passenger Agent......... 441 Sheidley Bldg
Kobe......... JAPAN.. J. Rankin, Agent................................ 14 A. Maye-Machi
Liverpool ...... ENG.. F. W. Forster, Agent....................... Royal Liver Building, Pier Head
London .... ENG.. H. S. Carmichael, General Passenger Agent...... 62-68 Charing Cross S. W.
.... T. S. Smith, General Freight Agent .... 67-68 King William St. E. C.
London .... ONT.. W. Fulton, City Passenger Agent................ 161 Dundas St.
Los Angeles ..... CAL.. A. A. Polhamus, General Agent, Passenger Department. 609 South Spring St.
Madrid .... SPAIN.. Thos. Cook & Son................................ 30 Calle de Arenal
.... International Sleeping Car Co.....14 Calle de Alcala, Equitable Bldg.
Melbourne ...... AUS.. Union S. S. Co. of New Zealand, Ltd.............
Minneapolis .... MINN.. W. R. Callaway, Passenger Agent, Soo Line....... 410 Nicollet Ave.
Montreal .... QUE.. A. E. Lalande, City Passenger Agent............. 238 St. James St.
.... E. J. Hebert, First Assistant General Passenger Agent. Windsor St. Station
Moscow .... RUSSIA.. International Sleeping Car Co.................... Hotel Metropole
Nelson .... B.C.. J. A. McDonald, District Passenger Agent........
New York....... N.Y.. W. H. Snell, General Agent Passenger Department.... 458 Broadway
.... International Sleeping Car Co.................... 281 Fifth Ave.
Niagara Falls .. N.Y.. D. Isaacs, Agent................................ Prospect House
Nice.......... FRANCE.. Thos. Cook & Son............................... 13 Promenade des Anglais
.... International Sleeping Car Co.................... 2 Avenue Massena
Ottawa .... ONT.. George Duncan, City Passenger Agent............. 42 Sparks St.
Paris......... FRANCE.. Aug. Catoni, Agent.............................. 1 Rue Scribe
.... Thos. Cook & Son................................ 1 Place d'Opera
Philadelphia ..... PA.. F. W. Huntington, General Agent, Passenger Dept...629-631 Chestnut St.
Pittsburgh ...... PA.. C. L. Williams, General Agent, Passenger Department. 340 Sixth Ave.
Portland .... ME.. Leon W. Merritt, Ticket Agent, Maine Central Railroad..... Union Depot
Portland ...... ORE.. F. R. Johnston, General Agent, Passenger Department,
.... Cor. Third and Pine Sts. (Multnomah Hotel)
Quebec........ QUE.. G. J. P. Moore, City Passenger Agent....... 30 St. John St., cor Palace Hill
Rome.......... ITALY.. Thos. Cook & Son............................... 54 Piazza Esedra di Termini
.... International Sleeping Car Co.............. 92 Place Sau Silvestro
Rotterdam .... HOLLAND.. Joh Otten & Zoon, Agents........................ Noordblaak 13
Sault Ste. Marie MICH.. W. J. Atchison, City Passenger Agent, W. C. Sutherland Depot Ticket Agent
St. John .... N.B.. W. B. Howard, District Passenger Agent.......... 8 King St.
St. Louis .... MO.. T. J. Barnes, City Passenger Agent............. 725 Olive St.
St. Paul ...... MINN.. L. M. Harmsen, City Ticket Agent, Soo Line...... 379 Robert St.
St. Petersburg RUSSIA. The Nordiska Resebureau, Agents.......... 19 Bolshaja Konjushenaja
San Francisco ... CAL.. G. M. Jackson, G. A. P. D................. 645 Market St. (Palace Hotel)
Seattle .... WASH.. E. E. Penn, General Agent, Passenger Department.... 713 Second Ave.
Shanghai ...... CHINA.. A. R. Owen, Agent..............................
Spokane .... WASH.. T. J. Wall, General Agent, Passenger Department.... 608 Sprague Ave.
Suva.......... FIJI.. Union S. S. Co., of New Zealand, Ltd...........
Sydney .... AUS.. Union S. S. Co. of New Zealand, Ltd............
Tacoma .... WASH.. C. H. Naylor, City Passenger Agent............. 1113 Pacific Ave.
Toronto .... ONT.. M. G. Murphy, Dist. Passenger Agt.: W. Maughan, C. T. A. 16 King St. East
Trieste ...... AUSTRIA.. P. Christofide, Agent.......................... Hotel De Ville
Vancouver ...... B.C.. H. W. Brodie, General Passenger Agent: J. Moe, City Ticket Agent.
Victoria .... B.C.. L. D. Chetham, City Passenger Agent............ 1102 Government St.
Vienna .... AUSTRIA.. S. Altman, Agent............................... Kaerntnerring
Warsaw .... RUSSIA.. International Sleeping Car Co...................
Washington ... D.C.. A. L. Powell, C. P. & P. A....Bond Bldg., 14th St. and New York Ave.
Winnipeg ...... MAN.. C. B. Foster, General Passenger Agent..... Cor. Main St. and Portage Ave.
.... A. G. Richardson, City Passenger Agent........... Hotel Bristol
Yokohama ..... JAPAN.. W. T. Payne, Manager Trans-Pacific Line......... 14 Bund

Messrs. THOS. COOK & SON, Tourist Agents, with offices in all parts of the world, are agents of the Canadian Pacific Railway, and can supply tickets and information.

1906512

A ROCKY MOUNTAIN BIGHORN

CANADIAN
PACIFIC
RAILWAY

Milton Keynes UK
Ingram Content Group UK Ltd.
UKHW022118070823
426486UK00005B/130